Pam Muñoz Ryan

Jennifer Strand

abdopublishing.com

Published by Abdo Zoom™, PO Box 398166, Minneapolis, Minnesota 55439.

Printed in the United States of America, North Mankato, Minnesota
062016
092016

Cover Photo: Pam Muñoz Ryan
Interior Photos: Pam Muñoz Ryan, 1, 5, 9; Seth Poppel/Yearbook Library, 6; Yuriya Gregoriyeva/Shutterstock Images, 7; iStockphoto, 8, 10, 14–15; Monkey Business Images/iStock, 11; Rita Kochmarjova/Shutterstock Images, 12–13; EPA European Pressphoto Agency B.V./Alamy, 14, 19; Christopher Futcher/iStockphoto, 16–17; Samuel Borges Photography/Shutterstock Images, 18

Editor: Emily Temple
Series Designer: Madeline Berger
Art Direction: Dorothy Toth

Publisher's Cataloging-in-Publication Data
Names: Strand, Jennifer, author.
Title: Pam Muñoz Ryan / by Jennifer Strand.
Description: Minneapolis, MN : Abdo Zoom, [2017] | Series: Amazing authors | Includes bibliographical references and index.
Identifiers: LCCN 2016941359 | ISBN 9781680792188 (lib. bdg.) | ISBN 9781680793864 (ebook) | 9781680794755 (Read-to-me ebook)
Subjects: LCSH: Ryan, Pam Munoz--Juvenile literature. | Authors, American--20th century--Biography--Juvenile literature. | Authors, American--21st century--Biography--Juvenile literature.
Classification: DDC 818/.5409 [B]--dc23
LC record available at http://lccn.loc.gov/2016941359

Table of Contents

Introduction

Pam Muñoz Ryan is a children's book author. She often writes stories about brave **heroines**. Her stories sometimes include Mexican-American **culture**.

Early Life

Pam was born on December 25, 1951. She grew up in California.

Her grandmothers lived in Oklahoma and Mexico. Pam liked to visit them. She also loved to read.

Rise to Fame

Pam became a teacher. She got married and became Pam Muñoz Ryan.

Then she had children.
Later she went back to school.

She wrote her first picture book. It was called *One Hundred Is a Family*.

It used counting to show different types of families.

Career

Ryan wrote her first **novel** in 1998. It was called *Riding Freedom*. Ryan did **research**. She used facts and her own ideas.

Pam Muños
Ryan

Her book *Esperanza Rising* is based on her grandmother's life. It won an award in 2002.

Legacy

Ryan's main characters are often females. They face challenges. But they work hard to solve them.

Ryan continues to write books.

She wants kids to love reading as much as she did.

Pam Muñoz Ryan

Born: December 25, 1951

Birthplace: Bakersfield, California

Husband: Jim Ryan

Known For: Ryan wrote *Esperanza Rising*. Many of her books are about brave heroines.

1951: Pam Muñoz Ryan is born on December 25.

1994: Ryan's first book is published.

1998: *Riding Freedom* is published.

2002: Ryan's book *Esperanza Rising* wins the Pura Belpré Medal.

2009: Ryan writes *Paint the Wind.*

2016: Her novel, *ECHO*, wins the Newbery Honor.

Glossary

culture - the way of living in a place at a given time. Culture includes a place's art, food, and customs.

heroines - women or girls who are the main characters in a story.

novel - a long written work that tells a made-up story.

research - careful study that is done to learn new facts or to solve a problem.

Booklinks

For more information
on **Pam Muñoz Ryan**, please visit
booklinks.abdopublishing.com

Zoom™ In on Biographies!

Learn even more with the Abdo Zoom
Biographies database. Check out
abdozoom.com for more information.

Index